LEGENDS FROM YORUBALAND

by

Kemi Morgan

Spectrum Books Limited

Ibadan • Owerri • Zaria

Spectrum Books Limited,
Sunshine House,
Second Commercial Road,
Oluyole Estate,
P M B 5612,
Ibadan.
Nigeria

In association with Safari Books (Export) Ltd
P O Box 316
Compendium House
1 Wesley Street
St. Helier
Jersey
Channel Islands

First published 1988

ISBN 978-246-003-6

Printed by Intec Printers Limited, Ibadan

Contents

Introduction

This collection of Yoruba legends is based on research works of eminent Nigerian scholars into the history, religion and culture of the Yorubas. Among these eminent Nigerian scholars were the late Rt. Rev. Samuel Ajayi Crowther, the first black Bishop, who preserved for us the story of Okanbi, and the Rev. Samuel Johnson, the historian, who gave us the story of Oduduwa. Others whose works have been used in the compilation of this book, were the Rev. T A J Ogunbiyi, an acknowledged authority on the religion of the Yorubas and the Rev. Lijadu of the Ondo Mission, whose research work on Ifa is now much sought after by present day scholars. Others were the late Rev. A B Akinyele, whose notes on the worship of Ogun in the Ondo Province form the basis of the story about Ogun, the god of iron and the late Sir Isaac Babalola Akinyele, who told the story of the origin of the ''Orun'' festival in Oyo in his book *Iwe Itan Ibadan*.

In compiling this book, the author is fully aware that there may be several versions of the stories told here and she would be only too glad to see these other versions collected together and made into books for the purpose of preserving them for posterity. For example, the author discovered that the many stories about the exploits of Ogun alone would make a book in itself and she has only selected one from among them which she considers suitable reading material for children. There are also many variations of the story of Ifa and the origin of Ifa and these variations too, when compiled together, can also make a book. It is to be hoped that our present day research scholars would apply themselves to this task.

It must be emphasized that in the compilation of these stories, the essential facts of the stories, as told by these men, have not been altered. But the style and the presentation have been changed to make them suitable reading material for the young.

To Parents and Teachers

This collection of Yoruba legends and folk-tales is intended for children in junior secondary school. It is intended to be used as a supplementary reader, and not as a prescribed textbook for examination purposes.

At the moment, there appear to be more textbooks for examination purposes on the market, and very few books for general reading. If we are to inculcate in our children, the habit of reading for pleasure and of gathering useful information, we must provide them with books which would interest them so much, that they would want to read them in their leisure hours.

Children have an insatiable curiosity for knowledge; they are always asking the questions why, when and how. They also have a vivid imagination and many of them live in a world of make-believe and fantasy. The world provides them with an escape from the humdrum and boredom of everyday life; and they see it, like Alice in Wonderland, through a magic looking-glass. In this magic world of children, live heroes, larger than life and villains worse than scoundrels. In this world too, animals and plants walk and talk and mingle freely with human beings, for it is a world without any form of barrier.

The purpose of this book then is to attempt to create for the children, a setting which will satisfy their instinctive tendencies and which will allow their emotions and imagination to run riot. The legends and folk-tales have been carefully selected to depict heroic exploits and daring adventures as well as to explain the reasons behind some of our social and cultural beliefs.

In the true manner of our oral tradition, children should be encouraged to learn and tell these tales. Parents and teachers can help them by asking questions.

If the reaction of the children to this book is to want to read more of such tales, then the author would have achieved her purpose in writing it.

Kemi Morgan

A Story of Ogun

Ogun is one of the gods worshipped in Yoruba land. He is the god of iron as well as the god of war. All Yoruba weapons of war and all implements of agriculture are dedicated to him. Some of these weapons are guns, swords, cutlasses, hammers, axes, and hoes. Legend says that Ogun was a man who lived in Ire, a town between Otankoto and Ikirun in Osun division. His father's name was Aje and his wife's name was Ija. Ogun and his wife had a son whose name has now been forgotten.

Ogun was a very fierce warrior and powerful magician. He knew how to make charms and how to cast spells on people. It is said that at one time, people became so afraid of him that they drove him out of the town into a dense forest. He had no cutlasses to cut his way through the forest and also no hoes to till the ground. He remained there helpless for seven days. Then, on the seventh day, he found a flint stone in the forest and he cast a spell on it. Immediately, a sharp sword came out of the stone and, with this sword, he cut a path through the forest and made his way back to his town.

When Ogun arrived back in town, he collected his followers together again and fought and won many battles against his enemies who had driven him into the forest. Then he made himself the

warrior chief of the town and became more powerful than ever. He had the largest collection of war weapons in Yoruba land and his fame as a great warrior with the magic sword spread far and wide. Wherever he went, a large crowd always gathered round him to see his famous sword.

At that time, there lived other warrior chiefs in the towns and villages near Ire. When they began to hear stories about Ogun's brave deeds and magical powers, they became jealous of him. "What is the world coming to?" asked one of them, "when a wild man like Ogun can gather such a crowd around him? We must do something to check him." So they began to plot to kill Ogun. They made secret arrangements with some of Ogun's enemies living at Ire to help them carry out their wicked plan.

One day, when Ogun and his family were busy working on their farm, a messenger ran to tell them that the town had been surrounded by enemies, who had come from far away and that there was panic among the people. Women and children were fleeing from their homes into the bushes around and the men were already hurrying back from their farms to defend their town. When Ogun heard the news, he became very wild. "How dare these fools attack our town?" he screamed. "I will teach them sense, yes, I will. By the gods of my fathers I swear, I will destroy them with my sword." And so saying, Ogun ran home to fetch his charmed sword with which he was determined to destroy the enemies.

After Ogun had gone to fight, some of his own townsmen who had purposely stayed behind, went and attacked his home. They found his son and killed him; but his wife and his father managed to escape into the forest. Then, the men set fire to his house and burnt it down. ''Now,'' they said, ''we have finished Ogun. He will never be able to live in this town again, even if he comes back safe from the battle.''

Ogun's presence at the battle front caused great fear in the hearts of the enemies and some of them ran away without fighting at all. Ogun fought bravely and with his charmed sword, slew many of his enemies and the rest fled in terror from the town. By sunset, the battle was over but Ogun decided to return home to his family the following morning, after a good night's rest.

In the morning, he set out for home in a very happy mood because he had won the battle and his town was safe again. As he walked along, he began to sing this song:

> 'Tis said, that Ogun cannot fight Oja,
> yet he fought Oja.
> 'Tis said that Ogun cannot fight Ewisi,
> yet he fought Ewisi
> 'Tis said that Ogun cannot fight Ireje,
> yet he fought Ireje
> Home

When he got near home, he met one of his relations weeping. He asked him why he was weeping, and the man told him the sad story of how his enemies in the town had plotted against him while he was away fighting. He told him how they killed his son and burnt down his house and how his father and his wife fled into the forest for safety.

Ogun was overcome with grief when he heard the news. He left the town and went to seek his father and his wife in the forest. He could not understand why his own people, for whose safety he had fought, should plot against him. He could not understand why anybody should want to kill his son. "What have I done to deserve this misfortune?" he kept asking himself, as he called on the gods of the land to punish the people for their wickedness.

Not long after Ogun left home, a terrible epidemic broke out in the town. People began to die like flies and the doctors were unable to find a cure for the small-pox epidemic. Soon, it began to look as if all the inhabitants of the town would die. So, the few remaining elders in the town decided to go and consult the Ifa oracle in Orunmila's house, to find out what they should do. "Surely the gods are angry with us. Let us go and find out what sacrifice we must offer to appease them," they said.

They consulted the Ifa oracle and the oracle told

them that the gods were angry with them because they killed Ogun's son. The oracle also told them that the epidemic would continue until Ogun and his family returned home.

The men returned in haste to their town to make arrangements for Ogun and his family to come back to live among them.

They sent emissaries to Ogun in the forest. When these emissaries got there, they begged Ogun to come home. They said, "We have suffered because of the crime we committed against you. Our town is laid waste by a strange disease, for which we can find no cure. Hundreds have died. The gods have surely punished us and they will continue to punish us unless you come back. Will you allow your own town, which you are always so ready to defend, to fall into ruins? Please come home, your people are anxious to welcome you back."

After much persuasion, Ogun agreed to go back and live in the town. "But," he said, "before I leave this forest, you must go and bring me a dog and a tortoise." The men did not know what he wanted to do with the dog and the tortoise but they were too afraid to ask him. So they went back to their town and brought the dog and the tortoise to him.

As soon as he got the animals, Ogun and his family set out for home. When they got near the gate leading to the town, Ogun commanded one of the messengers to kill the animals and to sprinkle their blood on the big toe of his right foot. "This must be done," he said, "to ward off the epidemic." The messenger did as he was told. Then Ogun and his followers entered the town.

A few days after Ogun got home, everybody became well and happy again. There was great rejoicing in the town. They made a great feast and, for many days, people sang and danced round the town to honour Ogun, their warrior chief.

However, six months later, Ogun died. The people wept and mourned him. They gave him a very grand funeral and afterwards made him a god and began to worship him. They collected his sword and other weapons of war together and kept them in a hut built of palm-fronds. To this day, such implements are always kept in huts in any place in Yoruba land where Ogun is worshipped. And also to this day, a dog is always sacrificed during the worship of Ogun, in rememberance of the blood of the dog sprinkled on Ogun's toe, to ward off the epidemic that once plagued Ire town.

The Story of Okanbi

Once upon a time, in a very far off country whose name has now been forgotten, there lived a king whose name was Okikisi. He was a great wizard who had strange magical powers which he always used to help people. He had a child whose name was Okanbi, meaning an only child. Okanbi was a brave and handsome boy who loved adventure. He was often found climbing rocks and hills trying to find out where the streams flowing down the hills came from. His father was very proud of him because he was brave, but he was also anxious about his safety because he was his only child. He did not want any harm to come to him. He wanted him to succeed him as king when he died.

It happened that at that time, Okikisi's kingdom was in great danger. The land was no longer fertile and every year the crops failed and food became very scarce. Okikisi was sad because he loved his people and did not want to see them starve. So, he called a meeting of all the wise men in his kingdom, to seek their advice on how to get food. At this meeting, they decided to send some men out to look for a fertile place where they could go and found a new settlement. They chose fifteen brave men to go in search of this new place. When Okanbi heard about the plan, he became interested and he begged his father to let him go with the men. At first, his father refused to let him go because he knew the journey would be long and dangerous.

And, as Okanbi was his only child, he did not want to endanger his life. But Okanbi continued to plead with him to let him go. He said to him, "Father, I know you love me very much; I know you do not want me to come to any harm and that you want me to become king after you. But this is the life I love! I seek adventure, and who knows where this one may lead me to? I may still become king where I am going and I may become so famous that the whole world will hear stories of my brave deeds. You, father, will be very proud of me too. Please, let me go." At last, the king, his father, agreed to let him go on the journey.

Among the sixteen people going on this journey were two men whom the king had chosen specially to look after his son during the journey. One of them was Tetu and the other was Okinkin, the king's own trumpeter. The king gave his son two very strange presents to take along with him on the journey. He gave him a small piece of black cloth with something tied up in it. He also gave him a cock. Then he called Okinkin the trumpeter, and said to him, "I choose you specially to go on this journey because I want you to look after my son and to see that no harm comes to him. Every time you are in danger or difficulty, blow your trumpet to tell my son to untie the small piece of black cloth which I have given him and you will immediately get help. Also, look after the cock, for the time will come when you will need its help

too."

At last, the day came when Okanbi and his men set out on their journey into the unknown. The sixteen men left the town and made for the forest. They were full of hope because they believed that in this forest, they would soon come to a suitable place where they could found a new settlement. But they were wrong. The forest they entered was a very inhospitable place. There was no sign of any human activity there. There were no houses, huts or farms anywhere. It was a thick forest, where giant trees, whose branches shut out the sun, grew. It was altogether a forbidding place. They stayed there for many days and nights, looking for a suitable place for a new settlement, but without success. They were often hungry, for they had only the few edible fruits and herbs growing there to eat. In the daytime, they found it difficult to walk quickly because their feet often got entangled among the creepers growing there. And at night, when they lay down on the bare ground to sleep, the sound of hyenas howling in the distance, the screeching of owls and other strange birds of the night, as well as the continuous humming of insects all night long, disturbed them. The journey was very uncomfortable but the men did not give up the quest, because they were determined to succeed.

After wandering in this forest for many days, they suddenly came to a place where they saw a very big river. They had never seen any stretch of water as big as that before, and they became very frightened. They had suffered hardships in the forest and they did not like the idea of going back through it again. But this river was big and probably deep and they had no boat to cross it. So they sat down on the bank of the river to plan what to do next. The brave Okanbi was the first to speak. He said: "Comrades, we have come a long way from home. We have suffered many hardships in the forest and we have not complained. If we return home now, people will call us cowards. But we are not cowards; we are brave men seeking a new and happy place for our people. Let us then, like brave men, enter this water and wade through it. If we die, nobody will call us cowards and if we live, we shall become great men whose brave deeds will be told to children on moonlight nights." With these brave words, Okanbi gave his men new hope and courage and they agreed to cross the river with him.

They entered the river and, as they waded through it, began to see slimy creatures of the water, like strange fishes and water-snakes, swimming past them. They became excited and began to talk about them. Soon it was noon; the blazing sun was now at its highest and had become a great ball of fire that shone remorselessly in the hot and copper sky. As the heat became intense, the men began to feel uncomfortable. And, as if to add more to their discomfort, there was the monotony of seeing nothing else besides the sky and water and the creatures living in it. Soon, discomfort gave way to a feeling of weariness; the men waded slowly on as if there was not enough strength left in them.

They were in this state of exhaustion when suddenly, the breeze dropped; the air became hot and stifling. Everything became still and silent and sad. Even the men did not speak to one another again. The eerie silence struck fear in their hearts because they recognized in it signs of an approaching tropical tornado. If there should be a heavy downpour of rain, they thought to themselves, the river would become swollen and they would all be drowned in it. The very thought of this happening horrified them, and they all, with the exception of Okanbi, began to lament their fate. They said they would never see their wives and children again and they began to call on the gods of their fathers to save them. Some began to grumble that Okanbi had brought them there to die and said that he should have told them to return home instead of asking them to cross the river with him. But Okanbi remained calm and silent. He never for a moment lost hope that they would come out of the river alive.

Just at this difficult moment, Okinkin remembered his trumpet and the king's advice to him before they left home. The king had said to him at the time, ''Okinkin, whenever you are in danger, blow your trumpet to remind my son to untie the small piece of black cloth which I have given him, and you will immediately get help.'' So, Okinkin quickly brought out his trumpet and blew it with all the strength that was left in him. Immediately Okanbi heard the sound of the trumpet, he remembered the piece of black cloth he had with him and he untied it. A palm-nut and some earth fell from the cloth into the river. All at once, right in the middle of the river, a palm-tree with sixteen palm-fronds sprang up on the spot where the earth and the palm-nut fell. The men were surprised to see the tree, and shouting and pointing in sheer amazement, they waded towards it. When they got there, they climbed to the top of the tree and rested on the palm-fronds. The cock also flew to the top of the tree and perched there.

After they had rested for a while on the tree, they began to think of the journey which was still before them. They did not know which way to go when they climbed down from the tree. Some said they should go east whilst others said they should go south. They could not agree amongst themselves whether to go east, west, south or north and they began to quarrel. Okikisi, the king, who was watching them from afar, saw what was happening and decided to go and help them. Being a wizard, he suddenly appeared to Okinkin and commanded him to blow his trumpet again. Okinkin obeyed him and blew his trumpet once again. Okanbi then again brought out the piece of black cloth which his father

18

gave him and some more earth fell from the cloth into the river. This time, the earth formed a small bank in the river. The cock was the first to see the small bank of earth in the river and he crowed loudly for joy and flew down from the tree and began to scatter the earth about. Wherever the earth touched water, the water dried up and became land.

When Okanbi saw the new land, he gave a shout of joy, and all his men joined him in giving this happy shout until the new land rang with the echoes of their voices. Then Okanbi, Tetu and Okinkin climbed down from the tree. At first, Okanbi refused to allow the rest of the men to climb down from the tree because they had grumbled when they were in danger. But the men begged for forgiveness and he forgave them and allowed them to climb down from the tree. Okanbi then told the men that he would allow them to live on the land only if they made him king and if each one of them promised to pay him a tax of two hundred cowries every year. The men agreed.

Okanbi called the new land Ife, and decided to settle there with his men. The land was very fertile and they grew plenty of food crops there. Soon, other people from their old home heard about their good fortune and they too came to join them in the new settlement. Before long, the settlement grew into a big town. Okanbi became a great and powerful king there and was loved and respected by all his subjects. He married and had seven children who became famous. The first child was a girl and she became the mother of the first Alaketu or king of Ketu. This Ketu was once a small but independent kingdom which lay between Agbome and River Ogun, south of the old Oyo kingdom. But it is now a town in the Republic of Benin. The other children were boys, and when they grew up, they became kings in different parts of Yorubaland. One became the first Orangun or King of Ila, another became the Onisabe or King of Sabe and yet another became the Olupopo or King of the Popos. The youngest was Oranyan and he became the most famous of all Okanbi's children. He was the mighty warrior who built a great Yoruba empire. The capital of this empire was old Oyo and the early Europeans who visited it called it Katunga. Okanbi himself lived to a good old age and died at Ife.

Foot-note: This story of the sixteen men that founded the new Ife explains why the Yorubas believe that originally there were sixteen obas in Yorubaland who are entitled to wear the beaded crown adorned with sixteen feathers of the sacred Okin bird.

Basorun, the Most Important Chief of Oyo

Basorun is a very important title in Oyo, and it is always given to the most senior councillor there. The title is given to a man who is believed to know all the secrets of heaven and people call him 'the keeper of heavenly secrets.' He is the chief priest who worships the god of fate. There is a festival in Oyo called Orun during which the god is worshipped. It is said that only the king, the Basorun and the king's mother know how this god is worshipped. Nobody else is let into the secrets of the worship of the god.

In olden times, the old Oyo empire was a great empire. It had its capital at Oyo-Ile and there, the king, called the Alaafin, lived in his beautiful palace which was adorned with one hundred brass posts.

At that time, the princes of Oyo were never allowed to live in the capital where their father lived. They were usually sent to live in other towns and villages that formed part of the empire so that they might learn how to rule the people.

It happened that there lived a prince of Oyo in one of these towns called Ikoyi. He was a very kind man and everybody in the town loved him. He was different from the other princes who had lived among them before, who were cruel and proud. This prince worked very hard to win the respect of the people of Ikoyi and to make the town a happy place for everybody to live in.

The prince was however unhappy because he had no children. The medicine-men in the town did their best to help him and his wife but they did not succeed. So, the elders of the town sent their messengers to other towns and villages of the empire to look for medicine-men who could help the prince. After a long search, they found one and brought him to the town. The medicine-man gave the prince and his wife some herbs and taught them how to use them. He said that he was sure that before the year ended, the prince's wife would give birth to a baby boy. The prince thanked the medicine-man and gave him many presents to take with him when he was returning home.

And true to the medicine-man's words, the prince's wife gave birth to a male child before the end of the year. There was great rejoicing in the town when the people heard the good news. They all went into the prince's house to see the new baby and to give him presents. They gave him strings of cowries, goats, hens, chickens, horses and foodstuffs like corn, yams, palm-oil and vegetables. In true Yoruba fashion, everybody gave the baby a name and nobody could tell how many names the baby had. The prince also made a great feast for the people and for many days, eating and drinking of palm-wine and dancing went on in the prince's house.

The child grew to be a very strong and handsome boy and everybody said, "At last, our prince has

got his own child who will be his heir." But when the boy was twelve years old, he died suddenly. The whole town was thrown into mourning. Everybody wept bitterly, and the prince was so overcome with grief that he planned to kill himself.

He left the town secretly and went straight into a dense forest to hang himself. Just as he was about to put a rope round his neck, he heard a voice calling out to him. The voice said, "What are you doing here? Who are you, for nobody ever comes here?" The prince was afraid when he heard the voice because he did not see anybody when he entered the forest. He began to tremble and the rope with which he wanted to hang himself fell from his hands. He then covered his face with his hands because he did not know whether the voice he heard was that of a human being or of a ghost. Then an old man, who was almost blind and who was clad in rags, appeared to him. The old man said to him, "I am the one speaking to you. I live all alone in this forest. I eat the fruits which I find here and I drink from the streams. I have heard your cries and though I am almost blind, I can see the rope with which you want to kill yourself. Now, tell me my son, why do you want to die?" The prince told the old man that he was tired of living because his only child whom he loved very dearly had died suddenly.

The old man listened patiently to the story of the prince and when he had finished, the old man said to him, "Son, do you know that you are not the only man who has suffered one way or another in this world? You have lost your child, I know, and you are very sad. But you are a prince; you are not a poor man who has nobody to look after him. You may even become king one day! Yet, there are people in the world who have lost everything they had and who are very poor. These people do not kill themselves. They still live in hope that some day, fortune will smile on them again."

Then the old man told the prince his own story. He said that he was once a very rich man who built a big and beautiful house. He had farms, horses, sheep, goats and plenty of cowries which was the money they used to spend at that time. He was so rich that he was able to feed and clothe a hundred relatives and servants, who lived in his compound.

Then one day, a terrible epidemic, which no one knew how to cure, broke out in the town. All the old man's relations and servants died as a result of this epidemic. His animals also perished; his farm was ruined and he lost his money and everything he had in the world. He was the only one left alive and there was nobody to comfort him or look after him. He wept so much that he became almost blind. In the end, he decided to go and live in a forest. He chose the one where the prince had now come to hang himself. He built a hut there and began to live there. The old man went on, "Son, I have never lost hope. I know that one day, fortune will smile on me again. I don't want you to lose hope either. Don't kill yourself. Go back at once to your town and when you get there, thank God and give alms to the poor. Better days are coming to you. Who knows, heaven itself, at this very moment, may be preparing great things for you. Go home, my son, go home at once because great things await you there.'' The prince was comforted by the old man's words and he thanked him and returned home.

When he got home, he found that everybody in the town had been looking for him. The king, his father, had died at Oyo and the king-makers had sent for him to make him king in his father's place. When the messengers from Oyo reached the town and the townspeople told them that they did not know where the prince was, they became very angry with them. They threatened to take all the men in the town to Oyo and put them in prison for failing to look after the prince. At that moment, the prince arrived back in the town. The people were so happy to see him back that they gave him a great welcome. Before the prince left the town for Oyo, he made a feast for the people and gave presents to all the beggars. When he had done this, he followed the messengers to Oyo where he was crowned king.

The prince did not forget the old man who had helped him in the forest. He sent his messengers to go and look for him in the forest and to bring him back to his palace. These messengers found the old man in his hut in the forest and they brought him to the palace at Oyo. The king was overjoyed to see his friend again. He gave him a house to live in, clothes to wear and plenty of food to eat. He also gave him servants to look after him.

A few days after the old man arrived in the palace, the king called his councillors together and told them about the old man who saved his life in the forest. He repeated what the old man had said to him in the forest. "Go home, my son, for heaven may be preparing great things for you. You may still become king, there is still hope for you." Then the king said to his councillors, "See how true the old man's words are! I owe my life to him. He is the one who changed my luck and told me I would become king. Let us then make him the chief priest of the god of fate so that he may always predict good for us."

The councillors agreed with the king and made the old man the chief priest of the god of fate. In Yoruba, this priest is called the 'Basorun'. After some years at Oyo, the old man regained his full sight and lived happily in the king's palace until he died.

After his death, the king and his councillors continued to choose a Basorun to be the chief priest of the god of fate. And up till now, you will find that the Basorun is the most important chief in Oyo and that the Orun festival when the god of fate is worshipped, is still celebrated there in the month of September.

Oduduwa, Lamurudu's Son

Once upon a time, there lived a man whose name was Oduduwa, the son of Lamurudu, a king who ruled in a place called Mecca. This Mecca is not the same one that the moslems go on pilgrimage every year. Nobody knows where the Mecca of this story really is, but some people say that it must be somewhere near Arabia. Others say that it must be part of a once all-powerful black kingdom of Meroe in Upper Egypt.

At the time when Lamurudu was king, the moslems began to come to Mecca to teach the people that there was only one God and that Mohammed was his prophet. As a result of this new teaching, some of the people, who were once pagans, threw away their idols and became moslems. They even built a mosque in the town.

Oduduwa did not like these moslems because he was a pagan. He worshipped other gods like the gods of the sun, the sky and the earth and he thought that if he did not drive away the moslems, they would become so strong that they would fight him and drive him out of Mecca.

So Oduduwa began to plan to prevent more people in Mecca from becoming moslems. He made friends with a man called Asara, who was a pagan priest and idol carver. These two men went and collected many idols together and they put them inside the mosque where the moslems worshipped.

Then Oduduwa told his people that they must all go to this mosque to pray to the idols. When the moslems heard about it, they were very angry because the mosque was their sacred place of worship, and they vowed that whenever an opportunity came their way, they would avenge this insult.

Asara, the pagan priest and idol maker had a son whose name was Braimoh. As a young boy, Braimoh had to go and sell his father's idols in the streets of Mecca. But he hated the work. So, when the moslems came and told the people that it was not good to worship idols, Braimoh was glad and he became a moslem secretly. His father, who did not know about his conversion to the moslem faith, kept on asking him to go and sell his carved idols for him. Everytime Braimoh went into the streets of Mecca to sell the idols, he would shout at the top of his voice, "Who wants to buy false gods! Who wants to buy false gods!" This always made his father very angry with him, and each time, he punished him. But the more his father punished him, the more he made up his mind that he would never bow down to an idol. He also vowed that if he ever had the chance, he would destroy all his father's idols and the idols in the mosque.

At last, Braimoh had the chance he had waited for, for so long. At that time, it was the custom in Mecca that before the yearly festival of the gods began, all the men in the town must go out to hunt for three days. In that year, Braimoh gave one reason or another why he could not go with the other men to hunt. And he stayed behind.

When all the men had left the town, Braimoh took his axe and went straight into the mosque where the idols were kept. One by one, he broke them into pieces with his axe. He left only the chief idol which looked like a very ugly man, standing. Around this idol's neck, he hung his axe so that everyone would know who destroyed the other idols. Then he left the mosque feeling very pleased with what he had done.

The three days set aside for hunting soon passed and all the men returned to the town to begin the festival of the idols. But when they went into the mosque to worship their idols, they found that all of them, except the ugly one, had been broken into pieces. Then they saw Braimoh's axe and knew that he was the culprit. They were very angry with him and they sent for him to ask him why he destroyed the idols.

When Braimoh came, they asked him, "Who did this wicked thing?" Braimoh, who was not sorry for what he had done, replied, making fun of them, "Why do you ask me? Can't you see that ugly one still standing there? Ask him who did it; can't he speak?" His judges replied, "Why do you ask us to speak to an idol? Can an idol speak?" "Why then do you worship something which can neither speak nor defend himself? Is that not a stupid thing

32

to do?'' Braimoh answered back. This made his judges so angry that they sentenced him to be burnt to death. For this purpose, they collected a thousand bundles of firewood and they also bought several pots of oil to set the firewood alight.

Whilst they were making this preparation to burn him to death, the other moslems in the town heard about it. They quickly came and rallied round Braimoh to save him. As soon as they got to the place where he was to be burnt to death, fighting broke out between them and the pagans. It was so serious that Lamurudu, the king, who was present at the scene of the fight, was killed. When the news of Lamurudu's death spread throughout the town, the pagans became afraid and many of them fled from the town.

Among those who fled from Mecca at the time were Oduduwa and two of his brothers. These two brothers travelled westwards from Mecca and later founded the kingdom of Gogobiri and Kukawa in the Hausa country. Up till today, the people who live in Gogobiri and Kukawa still dress like the Yorubas and have facial marks like Yorubas.

Oduduwa and his followers, however, travelled eastwards. Day after day, they trekked wearily on, stopping only at nightfall to sleep wherever night met them. There, they would light a fire to keep the wild animals and insects away and they would sleep with the sky above them as roof and the hard ground as bed. Most of the time they were travelling, they passed through arid lands where the ground was baked hard by the sun and where the very few trees that grew looked like gaunt old men that had been reduced to skeletons. Most of the area was thinly populated and water was very scarce. Very often, they had to trek several kilometers before they could get to one of the small settlements where there was a well. Here, if the inhabitants were friendly, they would stop for a night or two to rest and to refill their water skins before they continued their journey.

Sometimes, however, they passed through hostile settlements where the villagers attacked them with poisoned bows and arrows and chased them away. Some of them perished in these encounters with hostile villagers. The rest however, trudged on, in the hope that one day they would come to a hospitable place where they could settle permanently.

After many days of travelling, they left the arid lands behind and entered a forest area. Here, they found the ground carpeted with the greenest grass that anyone could imagine; and here too, they saw thick shady trees growing in abundance and rivers flowing. Here and there, they saw dotted farms where corn and vegetables were planted and they guessed that they must be near some big, well established settlements. The thought that they had reached a fertile area where they could settle permanently, filled Oduduwa and his followers with joy and they gave thanks to their gods who had brought them so far. They saw many bush paths leading to these settlements and they followed one of them. As they went along, they met some farmers from the settlement going to their farms.

At the sight of them, the farmers fled back to their settlement to warn the others to run and take shelter in the bushes around them because strangers of noble bearing were coming to their settlement to enslave them. So the settlement was deserted when Oduduwa and his followers first arrived there.

However, Oduduwa's men caught one of the farmers as he was running away. By sign language, they spoke to him and assured him that they were friends from a far off country seeking a place to settle. "And what is the name of your settlement?" they asked him. The man replied by sign language, "Ife, Oyelagbo." Then he continued, "The place where you now stand is called Ijio and it is only from here you can enter Ife Oyelagbo." "And who is your king?" asked Oduduwa. The man replied, "He is the divine one and lives many days journey from here. There, in his great kingdom, he holds his court." Oduduwa asked him again, "How does one get to the town of your great king?" The man simply replied, "I do not know." then he asked him again, "What is your name?" The man did not reply. Then finally Oduduwa asked him, "What is the name of the tribe that lives in this settlement?" He replied, "We are Igbo."

Oduduwa then asked him to escort them from this junction where they stood and which is now known as Ijio road, to Ife Oyelagbo.

And so, after ninety days of suffering and long treks, Oduduwa and his followers came to Ife. There, they found the houses deserted and they entered them and began to live in them. But the Igbos, who had fled into the bushes began to harass Oduduwa and his followers. They would cover themselves up with raffia and come back to Ife town to frighten Oduduwa's people and carry them away as slaves. It was not until later that a woman called Moremi learnt the secrets of the Igbo people and saved Oduduwa's people from them.

The moslems at Mecca were not happy that Oduduwa and his followers escaped. So they sent an army under the command of a soldier called Sahibu to go and fight Oduduwa at Ife. But when they got there, Oduduwa and his men defeated them and they captured from them what many people think is a copy of the Koran. the Koran is the moslem Bible. This particular Koran is called 'Edi' in Yoruba and it means 'something tied up'. It is kept in a sacred place at Ife and it is worshipped till today.

Oduduwa and his followers settled down happily at Ife and other people came and joined them there. He became a great king at Ife and he is regarded as the great ancestor of the Yoruba people.

Oduduwa never forgot that he entered Ife through

the Ijio road. He built a shrine there and appointed one of his trusted servants called Orajioye to go and live there and look after the shrine and protect all those who settle near him. He also decreed that all those who would succeed him as rulers of Ife must always be taken, at their coronation, to this junction. Here, the Chief Obajio who is in charge of this shrine would remind the new ruler now called 'Ooni', of how his ancestor, Oduduwa, entered Ife for the first time through the Ijio road. These are the actual words the Obajio would use in telling the new Ooni how Oduduwa came to Ife:

"This is the route by which your father, Oduduwa, entered Ife and my father Orajioye was his trusted servant. It was your father who placed my father here and therefore all the women and children of this quarter are yours and should be protected by you."

How The Egungun Festival Began

In Yoruba land, there is a festival which is called the *Egungun* festival. The Yorubas believe that the spirits of their ancestors always return to earth to bless them. In some towns like Ibadan, the festival always takes place around June when new food crops have just come out and food is plentiful and cheap. People from the farms and villages come home for the celebration and there is usually great rejoicing in the town.

Each family has its own *Egungun* who represents the spirit of its ancestor. These *Egunguns* must cover themselves up so that no part of their bodies will be seen when they are dancing in the streets or performing magical acts to entertain people. They wear masks to cover their faces and when they speak, they make strange noises. The town of Ibadan also has its own *Egungun* whose duty it is to bless the Olubadan and all the people of Ibadan. He calls on all the spirits of the rivers and streams in Ibadan to bring good fortune to the town. He prays for good harvest, good health and peace throughout the year.

"How did the *Egungun* festival begin?" asked a stranger who once saw the *Egunguns* dancing in a Yoruba town during the festival. An Ifa priest who stood near the stranger replied with a riddle:

"The dance of an *Egungun* has neither rhyme
nor rhythm;

The joys of a spoilt child can be a perennial source of annoyance to others; for excessive are the demands of a spoilt child.

If you train your child properly,
he will learn to behave properly,
If you do not train him properly,
he will become as stupid and as useless as a
yam that is not well cooked.''

The stranger was puzzled by this riddle and he begged the priest to explain it to him. So the priest told him this story.

''Once upon a time, there lived a woman who had a child whose name as Ojulari. Ojulari was a spoilt child who always did what he liked. His mother was afraid to scold him, because all her other children had died and she was anxious that Ojulari should live.

One day, Ojulari took his mother's cloth and covered his face and body with it and began to dance. He was in a very happy mood that day. His mother sat on a low wooden stool watching him dance, and she was amused. Soon, Ojulari asked her to beat the stool she sat on, like a drum, and to sing for him whilst he danced. His mother agreed and she began to beat the stool she sat on, like a drum, while the child danced. When he became tired, he fell asleep.

Ojulari enjoyed himself so much that day, that

when he woke up the following morning, he covered himself up again with his mother's cloth and began to dance. Then he went and asked his mother to beat her stool again like a drum while he danced. But his mother was very busy then, and she refused. She told him to go outside and play with the other children in the neighbourhood.

Ojulari was very angry with her and he flew into a rage. He threw himself on the ground and began to weep bitterly. His mother took no notice of him and said to herself, "My son will soon forget about the dance and will stop crying when other children come to play with him." But Ojulari did not stop crying and he refused to play with the other children in the neighbourhood.

The following day, Ojulari became ill with fever. His mother, remembering that all her other children had had fever and died, became alarmed. She ran to an Ifa priest who consulted the oracle for her. The oracle told her that if she wanted the child to get well, she must give him everything he asked for. The woman thanked the Ifa priest and ran home.

As soon as she got home, she made a sack for the boy to cover himself up with. Then she sat on her wooden stool and began to beat it like a drum. She was not a good drummer, but as soon as he heard his mother beating her stool like a drum, Ojulari got up from his sick bed and began to dance. His mother gave him the sack she made for him to cover himself up with and he was very pleased with it. He wore it and danced until he was tired. Soon after, the fever left him and he was well again.

Everyday, the boy continued to ask his mother to beat her stool like a drum whilst he danced. His mother dared not refuse him because of what the Ifa priest told her. She had no time to do her own work and very often she had to stay up late into the night to get any work done. Ojulari became a real nuisance to his mother. He began to ask her to give him food to eat after every dance and she had to stay nearby whilst he ate the food, to drive away the goats that came to share his food with him.

Ojulari's mother found that cooking meals at odd times was a great strain on her. So she thought of a plan. She would always have food which she could cook before hand for the boy to eat. She would always have *eko*, a kind of porridge made with corn, and *moyinmoyin*, a kind of steamed pudding made with beans, ready for her son. She also bought whips. She gave them to him and taught him how to use them to drive away the goats.

When Ojulari grew up to be a man, he became responsible and sober, and was very sorry for all the trouble he gave his mother when he was young. He stopped dancing and learnt a useful trade. But, by that time, his mother had grown old and feeble.

and it was not long before she died.

Ojulari was very sad to lose his mother; he made a promise that he would always have a celebration in her memory. This was what he did. He invited all his friends to the first celebration. He gave them *eko* and *moyinmoyin* to eat, just as his mother used to give him to eat when he was young. After food, he gave them sacks to cover themselves up with and invited them to join him in a dance through the streets of the town. He told his drummer to beat his drum just as his mother used to do. His mother, who was not a drummer, beat her stool anyhow in those days. Now, the real drummer who beat a proper drum for Ojulari and his friends had to pretend that he too did not know how to beat a drum. He beat it anyhow like Ojulari's mother.

The drum is called the *Bata* drum and its rhythm is irregular to make it sound like Ojulari's mother's drum. All *Egunguns* dance to its irregular rhythm till today. Ojulari also remembered the goats that used to trouble him when he ate his food and the whip his mother gave him to drive them away. So, Ojulari and his friends also carried whips in their hands when they danced round the town, with their faces and bodies completely covered up. This was Ojulari's idea of a memorial for his mother.

Every year, Ojulari continued to remember his mother in this strange way and when he grew old and died, his own children continued to remember him and their grandmother in the same way every year.

The idea of having a memorial for one's relations in this manner soon spread throughout Yoruba land and it became known as the '*Egungun* festival'. Ojulari, who first started this memorial for his mother is now called the father of all *Egunguns*. After some time, this simple memorial became an important religious affair. It became the worship of one's ancestors who, every year, return to earth to bless their relations and townsmen.

Some of the most beautiful pieces of poetry in Yoruba may be found in the chants of the *Egunguns* as they dance around the streets of a town. It is a pity that they cannot be translated into English without losing some of their true Yoruba poetic beauty. Here is an example of one of them. It is like a lullaby:

> *Mo de were bi eji ale,*
> *Mo de kesi bi eji owuro,*
> *Mo de pa-pa-pa bi eji iyaleta;*
> *Mo de k'oloko ma le r'oko,*
> *Mo de k'omode ma le r'odo,*
> *Mo de k'omode ma le sunkun omu,*
> *Omo kansoso ni mo mu w'aiye; kuru!*

This is the English translation:

> *I come softly as the showers at night;*
> *I come early as the dew at dawn;*
> *I come quickly as the showers at sunrise;*

I come to stop farmers from going to farm;
I come to stop her that goes to the stream at dawn;
I come to stop children from crying for the breast;
Behold I come into the world with an only child!

Imeren and Molarin

Once upon a time, there lived a woman and her daughter and step-daughter. Her daughter's name was Molarin and her step-daughter's name was Imeren. Their mother spoilt Molarin. She never scolded her because she believed she could never do anything wrong. Imeren was always blamed for everything they did wrong. She always accused her of bringing misfortune to them.

One day, the mother went out to visit her relations. Before she left, she asked the girls to scrub the wooden bowl they used to collect water. When she was washing it, Molarin dropped the bowl and broke it. Then their mother arrived and saw the broken bowl. She at once began to scold Imeren for breaking it. Imeren told her mother that it was Molarin who broke it, but she refused to listen to her and accused Imeren of telling lies against her sister. Imeren was so sad that she began to cry. Her step-mother, in a sudden fit of temper, brought out her stick and began to beat Imeren. Imeren ran out of the house, crying as she ran along. Their mother did not bother to call her back because she thought she would soon come back when she was hungry. But Imeren never came back.

The next day, when Imeren had still not returned, the woman became alarmed and she organized a search party to look for her. But she vowed that

when Imeren returned, she would punish her for causing all of them so much trouble. The search party went from house to house to look for her. They combed the surrounding bushes but Imeren was not there. They went to nearby farms and junctions of roads and asked if anybody had seen her. But nobody had. When they were tired, they called off the search and returned to their homes. They thought that when Imeren was tired, she would find her way back home. But Imeren never came back.

Not long after she ran away from home, her stepmother and her sister, Molarin, went to the river to fetch water. On their way to the river, they began to talk about the strange disappearance of Imeren until they got to the river-side. They put down their pots from their heads and wanted to start filling them with water. All of a sudden, they heard a loud voice from nowhere saying, "Who is calling Imeren? Molarin broke the bowl yet you said it was Imeren, who broke it. Imeren now lives in a deep deep forest; deep, deep down a swamp, where the sponge plant grows and bears fruit in abundance!" Then, the voice broke into a song.

The woman and her daughter were startled when they heard the voice and the song from nowhere. They left their pots by the river-side and ran home to tell their neighbours about this strange incident. Their neighbours followed them to the river and they too heard the voice and the song from nowhere and they also ran away from there in great fear.

Soon, news reached the king about this strange happening. So he and his chiefs also went to the river. There, they too heard the voice and the song. They too became afraid and ran home.

When they got home, the king sent for the wisest man in the town, who had a big head and one leg. He hobbled to the palace. When he got there, the king told him about the voice and the song that came from nowhere which they heard near the river. The king then sent him to the river to find out where the voice and the song came from. The man went to the river.

As soon as he got to the river-side, the strange voice began to speak. "Why are you all calling Imeren, Imeren? It was Molarin who broke the bowl yet you said Imeren broke it! Imeren now lives, deep, deep in a forest far away; deep, deep down in the swamp where the sponge plant grows and bears fruit in abundance." Then the voice again started to sing a sad song.

The wise man did not run away when he heard the voice and the song. He stood there, deep in thought. Then suddenly he began to talk in a loud voice. He called out Imeren's name three times and then assured her that nobody would ever blame her again for breaking the bowl for the truth was out. Then he commanded her never to speak or sing again at the river-side because she now belonged to the spirit world and there she should stay and sing and dance and be happy for ever. The voice and the song stopped immediately. And ever since that time, nobody has ever heard Imeren speak or sing again because her spirit is at peace. But the river is still called the Imeren River.

The Tortoise and the Elephant

Once upon a time, a certain king had a dream which frightened him. He dreamt that evil would befall him. So he sent for all the wise men in his kingdom to come and interpret the dream for him. They came and told him what his dream meant. They told him that he would die suddenly unless he offered a live elephant as a sacrifice.

The king was worried because he knew that it would not be easy to capture an elephant alive. So he sent for all the hunters in his kingdom. When they came, he told them that anyone of them who captured an elephant and brought it to him alive, would be rewarded with half of his kingdom. The hunters knew that this was an impossible mission, but they were afraid to tell the king the truth. So they made false promises to the king that they would bring him the elephant very soon. Then they left the king and returned to their homes.

The king waited for the hunters to return, but they never came back. The king was so angry with them that he swore that before he died, he would kill all of them.

In the meantime, the tortoise had heard of the king's predicament. So he went to the king and swore to him that he would bring him a live elephant within seven days. The king was pleased to hear the news and he promised to give the tortoise half of his kingdom if he did so. The tortoise then gave the king the following instructions. He said the king should order his men to dig a big and deep trench in the market square. He said the king was also to buy many beautiful mats fit only for kings. On the morning of the seventh day, the mats were to be carefully spread to cover the trench, and should also be cleverly arranged so that the top would look like a king's throne. No one should suspect that there was a trench beneath the mats. Lastly, he told the king that all his people were to assemble at the market square on the morning of the seventh day. They were to come along with clubs and cutlasses cleverly hidden under their garments. When they arrived at the square, they were to sit around the trench covered with the mats, to wait for the tortoise.

After giving the king these instructions, the tortoise said goodbye to him and asked him to expect him on the seventh day at the market square.

As soon as the tortoise left the king, he went and bought roasted groundnuts then went home. He ground the nuts into a smooth paste and then mixed the paste with honey. This, he made into sweet balls, which he packed into a bag. Early in the morning of the seventh day, he slung the bag across his shoulder and set out with the bag for the forest of elephants.

He soon reached the forest of elephants, where he saw a big elephant that had eaten too much, and was resting under a big Iroko tree. He looked tired and half asleep and was not in a fighting mood. The tortoise, however, approached him cautiously. When he came within a short distance of him and saw that the elephant was watching him, the tortoise began to speak. He prostrated on the ground and began to put sand on his head in an act of submission to the elephant. Then he said to the elephant, "My lord of the forest; my lord of the plains; the only mighty one that shakes the mighty forest; I adore you; I worship you and pledge my loyalty to you." The elephant was surprised to see the tortoise behaving in this manner and he asked him what he wanted from him. The tortoise then told him that he had brought a very important message to him from far, far away. "But", said the tortoise, "I pray your majesty will first of all accept this humble gift from your obedient servant before your obedient servant delivers the message to your majesty." The tortoise then gave the elephant a few of the sweet groundnut balls to eat. The elephant liked them and asked for more. The tortoise was pleased and gave him a few more.

Whilst he was eating and enjoying the sweet groundnut balls, the tortoise delivered the message to him. He told him that the king of his town had died and that all the people of his town had agreed to make the elephant their king because he was the only one who could protect them and rule them well. He told him that his townsmen had already made a throne for him in the market-place, where

l sit and judge them. He also told him that
eople had assembled in the market-square
me him as their new king. The elephant
was flattered. He agreed to go with the tortoise.

The two of them set out for the town of the
tortoise. As they went, the tortoise began to feed
the elephant with more sweet groundnut balls. He
also began to sing that he was taking the elephant
to heaven and that hunters would dance, dance,
dance. The elephant did not care to listen to the
words of the song but kept on eating sweet
groundnut balls.

As they were about to leave the forest of
elephants, the guard-elephant whose duty it was
to warn others of any danger, saw them. He was
very suspicious because none of the other animals
trusted the tortoise. He was a wicked and cunning
animal. He felt that the tortoise was up to one of
his tricks. So, he began to blow his trumpet to warn
his brother elephant not to follow the tortoise. But
his brother elephant did not listen to the warning
because he was too busy eating sweets.

At last, the tortoise and the elephant reached the
town. The tortoise led him to the market square
where the people were sitting, waiting for them.
The people gave a shout of joy when they saw them
coming and the tortoise said to the elephant, "See
how glad the people are to see their king! I will
leave you now and let you go and sit on your
throne. See how beautiful the throne is." The

elephant was so flattered by the shouting and crying, that he raised his head proudly, and waved his trunk to the people. They clapped harder as he stepped, smiling, on the mats covering the trench. In a flash, the mats gave way and the elephant fell inside the deep trench. The people immediately got up, ran to where the elephant lay in the trench, and clubbed him to death there.

And so ended the tragic tale of the foolish, proud and greedy elephant. His carcass was offered as a sacrifice by the people to save their king's life. The tortoise was also rewarded for being so clever.

Kiigbo — The Disobedient Boy

Once upon a time, there lived a boy. He lived with his parents in a little hut built near farm lands. His father was a good farmer. He was very hard working. But Kiigbo, his son, was a problem child. He was very restless and never settled down to do anything properly. Besides, he was bad-tempered and wilful. He would never take advice; no, not even from his father. He never obeyed any instruction given to him. His parents tried their best to make him change his ways but he refused to change. They reasoned with him, begged him, cajoled him and at times threatened him, to make him change his ways, but he did not change. So they left him to face the consequences of his actions. They told him the Yoruba proverb which says that a child who refuses to take instruction at home will be taught a bitter lesson by strangers when he leaves home.

One day, Kiigbo told his father that he wanted to go and start his own farm, away from his father's farm. His father was pleased because he thought that his son was becoming more serious and wanted to settle down. So, he began to advise him. The first advice that he gave to him was that if he came to any land which had never been cultivated by anybody before and where no palm-trees or kola-nut trees grew, he should avoid that land because it was a sure sign that the land belonged to the spirits. And the spirits were wicked spirits that killed people. Kiigbo thanked his father for his advice and promised never to go on spirit land to farm.

A few days later, Kiigbo left home in search of abandoned farm land to establish his own farm. As he walked along, he came to a large piece of vacant land. There were no huts or cultivated farms near it. There were no palm trees or kola-nut trees near it. The whole land looked deserted. The eerie silence in the place was enough to make anybody afraid but not Kiigbo. He said to himself, "So this is the earth-spirits' land my father told me about? Well, I see no spirits around! I think it is the silence that frightens people away from here. But I, Kiigbo, I am not a coward; I am going to start my farm here; and I swear, a thousand spirits cannot prevent me from doing so."

So, Kiigbo went on the land and started to cultivate it. He began to till the land with his hoe. As he was working, he heard the sound of many voices calling out to him and asking him what he was doing. He was not afraid, and without even looking up to find out who were speaking to him, he simply replied in a loud voice, "It's me Kiigbo; I am tilling the land. I am going to start my farm here."

The voices replied, "Oh, if that's all you are doing, we'll help you. We will always help you do anything you want to do on the farm." In a twinkling of an eye, the whole place was filled with earth-spirits carrying hoes. They began to help Kiigbo to till the ground. In no time at all, they finished clearing the whole land for Kiigbo. Kiigbo was astonished at the speed with which they worked and he was pleased with them and thanked them. Laughing a horrible laugh, the spirits said good bye to him and disappeared into nowhere.

He congratulated himself for disobeying his father and for finding this land where he got labour for nothing. There, and then, Kiigbo reached out for his bag and brought out the seeds he wanted to plant in the land. As soon as he started putting the seeds into the ground, the voices came again calling to him and asking him what he was doing there. Kiigbo replied again, "It's me, Kiigbo, your friend. I am planting my corn." So the spirits trooped out again and in no time helped him to plant his corn. Then they disappeared.

Kiigbo felt very pleased with himself. He sat down on the ground to rest for a while and whilst he was resting, he began to think of how rich and famous he would become when his corn ripened and he harvested it and sold it. He had become impatient. He wanted the corn to grow fast and to ripen quickly. Still busy with his thoughts, he fell asleep. For how long he slept, he did not know. But when he woke up, he saw that all the corn he planted that morning had sprouted up and that the corn-sheaves had already appeared and were almost ready for harvesting. Kiigbo's eyes almost

fell out of their sockets when he saw this miraculous sight. He then said, greatly astonished, "Who would believe that I started cultivating this land this morning! Surely, I, Kiigbo, am born lucky! Maybe, I will stay here till I harvest my corn so that thieves may not come to steal it."

Instead of going home for the night, he stayed on the farm to watch his corn. By evening time, the corn had ripened and was ready for harvesting. So Kiigbo got up again and began to pluck the ears of corn. As soon as he started, the voices came again. They asked, "What are you doing Kiigbo?" He replied, "My corn is ripe and I want to pluck some to take home to show my father. Later, I will come back again to harvest the rest and sell it so that I may become rich." Once more, the spirits came out again to help Kiigbo harvest his corn. But instead of plucking some of the corn and leaving the rest, they plucked all and destroyed them. And laughing a hideous laugh, they disappeared.

Kiigbo took one look at the destruction on the farm and began to weep and to beat his head with his hands, blaming himself for disobeying his father. The spirits heard him hitting himself on the head with his hands and they came out again and said to Kiigbo, "We'll help you to hit yourself as well." So they all crowded round him and beat him to death.

The Story of Jigbo

Once upon a time, there lived a king whose name was Oluwo. He had a son whose name was Jigbo. Jigbo was a very brave boy. Everybody loved and admired him for his courage and bravery. His parents therefore thought that he would make a good soldier and they began to plan for him to become the head of his father's army when he became a man. But Jigbo was not interested in becoming a soldier. He wanted to be a hunter. His parents begged him to change his mind, but he refused to do so. In the end, they agreed to let him become a hunter. His parents gave him a fine horse to ride on his hunting expeditions.

The time soon came when Jigbo set out on his hunting expedition. On the first day, he rode his fine horse into the forest of elephants and buffaloes. He did very well that day. He killed many animals and brought their carcases home in the evening, to the delight of his parents and his friends. Before long, the fame of Jigbo as a brave hunter spread far and wide. Soon, other hunters began to join him on these hunting expeditions. And each time they went, they returned home with plenty of game.

But one day, tragedy struck. As they chased the animals deeper and deeper into the forest, the clouds began to gather. Soon, a tropical thunderstorm followed and there was a torrential downpour. In the confusion that followed this downpour, Jigbo lost his way in the darkness. He later found himself and his horse swept by the torrent into a deep ditch. The horse had died. There Jigbo lay, helpless and feeble for three days. On the third day, the tortoise passed by the ditch and saw Jigbo inside it. So, he went and found a rope and threw it to Jigbo and asked him to climb on the rope to safety. Jigbo did so. But as soon as Jigbo came up, the tortoise seized him, threw him inside his drum and imprisoned him there. He made a small hole in the drum through which he fed Jigbo to keep him alive. Then he went on his way home.

When they reached home, the tortoise commanded Jigbo to sing each time he started beating the drum. Jigbo agreed to do so. To test whether Jigbo would obey him or not, he took the drum with Jigbo inside it and slung it across his shoulder. Then, in a loud voice, he said to the drum, "My own drum: my own drum; do you hear me? Begin to sing now!" Immediately, Jigbo began to sing that he was the son of Oluwo, that his parents gave him a horse to ride on his hunting expeditions, that he hunted in the forest of elephants and buffaloes. But alas! he was washed away by torrential rain and that was how he became the slave of the tortoise. The song was so melodious that even the tortoise began to dance to it. When he stopped dancing, he laughed.

"This drum will make me rich! From now on, I am going from town to town to beat my drum to entertain people and to collect money from them.

This surely will make me rich!"

The tortoise at once set out to visit these towns and villages to entertain the people there with his drum. Wherever he went, he pulled a large crowd of people who came to dance to the music of his singing drum. He soon became rich and his fame spread far and wide. Soon, he began to get invitations from many towns and villages asking him to come and entertain the people there with his drum. He always went, but would never let the drum out of his sight.

In the meantime, Oluwo, the king and Jigbo's father, had given up all hope of ever seeing his son alive again. He was very sad, but when he heard of the tortoise and his drum, he thought he would invite him to come to his town to entertain him and make him happy. The tortoise accepted the invitation, not knowing that the king, Oluwo, was Jigbo's father.

When he got to Oluwo's town, the tortoise went to the palace where a large crowd had gathered to listen and dance to the music of his drum. As usual, the tortoise commanded his drum to start singing. Then the drum began to sing.

Jigbo, Jigbo, son of Oluwo
Agbamurere;
Jigbo, Jigbo, son of Oluwo
Agbamurere.
Father gave me a horse to ride to hunt;

Mother gave me a horse to ride to hunt;
I hunted in the forest of buffaloes and
elephants;
But alas! the torrential rain swept me into a
ditch
And this was how I became the slave of the
tortoise.
Kiriji, kiriji, kenkeluke
Agbamurere.

As soon as the people heard the music, they began
to dance. The sound was so wonderful that even
the king was not left out. He too began to move
his feet, without listening to the words . But there
was an old chief there who did not dance. He was
more interested in the words of the song. Could
Jigbo, our son, whom we are looking for, be the
one inside the drum, he asked himself. When the
dancing stopped, the chief went and told the king
about his suspicion. The king was taken aback by
this news. He and the chief began to plan how to
get at the truth of the matter. They called the
tortoise and thanked him for entertaining them so
well. They placed plenty of food and plenty of
intoxicating drinks before him and asked him to
eat and drink and enjoy himself. Now, the tortoise
was a greedy person. He kept the drum safe beside
him, and he ate and ate, and drank and drank so
much, that he became dizzy and tired and fell into
a deep sleep.
  While he was snoring, the king and his chief

carefully took the drum of the tortoise and opened it and they found Jigbo, their lost son, inside it. They were so happy to see him again, but were sad when they saw that he had become very thin and ill. They took him away, then they sewed the drum up again.

When the tortoise woke up, they asked him to entertain them with his drum. He did not know that they had opened the drum and had taken Jigbo away from inside it. The tortoise commanded the drum to start singing, but no sound came from it. In desperation, the tortoise began to curse and swear at the drum; but still no music came from it. Then he became afraid and began to tremble. The king asked the tortoise in a deep angry voice, ''Why is your drum not singing again?'' The tortoise did not reply. Then the king called Jigbo to come and meet the tortoise. When the tortoise saw Jigbo, he was frightened! He wanted to run away, but the guards grabbed him and brought him before the king. There and then, in the presence of everyone, the king commanded that the tortoise be put to death.

A Story of Ela

In Yoruba legends, *Ela* was a young god in heaven. *Olodumare*, the supreme god of the Yorubas, loved him very much. He sent him down from heaven to earth to help him in his work of creation at Ife, the garden of Eden of the Yorubas. For this reason, the Yorubas regard him as being next in rank to Olodumare.

At that time, Ela spent seven days on earth creating all things out of the dark and stagnant waters that then covered the whole earth. He created the dry land; he created the oceans, rivers and lakes; he created the hills; he created the animals and fishes and caused the plants to grow. Then he created men to live on earth. When he finished his work, he climbed back to heaven on a rope.

But while Ela was busy creating all the good things on earth, *Esu,* another powerful god in heaven, was busy waging war against Olodumare. He was angry with Olodumare because Olodumare had not chosen him to go down to earth to create life there. So he declared war on Olodumare. But Olodumare defeated him and the other rebel gods who had joined him. Olodumare drove them out of heaven. After their defeat, they came down to earth to fight Ela and to prevent him from doing his work. But Ela also defeated them.

After Ela had gone back to heaven, Esu and his followers decided to live on earth to cause confusion among the peoples of the earth. And so, it happened that each time Esu and the rebel gods caused trouble on earth, Olodumare would send Ela down to earth to restore order. Each time Ela was sent back to earth, he came as a human being; and each time, he had a different name and different parents. His other names were *Orunmila, Oluorogbo* and *Agbonniregun*. Because of the nature of the duties Ela was performing on earth, the Yorubas regarded him as the greatest restorer of peace and order on earth and their priests used to say to him:

> Ela, thou child of Agbonniregun.
> Ela, thou great restorer of peace.
> Ela, thou child of Ogun,
> Ela, thou giver of good gifts
> Once destruction threatened the land of Ife,
> 'Twas Ela that came and restored order there.
> Once rebellion broke out in the land of Akila,
> And there was confusion everywhere;
> 'Twas Ela that came and restored order there.
> Once darkness enveloped the land of
>   Okerekere
> And day was turned to night;
> 'Twas Ela that came and brought light.
> Once Satan waged a war on earth,
> And turned the whole place upside down,
> 'Twas Ela that came and restored order there.
> Ela takes no money, Ela takes no gifts,

Ela only gives good gifts to men.
He made Odundun, king of the leaves;
He made tete its next in rank;
He made the ocean, the king of waters;
He made the lagoon its next in rank.
Still, men found fault with Ela's works,
Till Ela in desperation, hooked up his cord,
to heaven,
And on it ascended back to heaven.
Men now seek Ela
But find him not;
For there'll be none like him again. Men now
cry; 'Oh; Ela
Wilt thou not return to bless?
Wilt thou not come to restore order on earth
again?'

Here is one of the many stories about Ela. Once upon a time when Ela was on earth, gods and men dwelt together at Ife. At that time, he was called Orunmila. He used to go from place to place teaching people how to grow new crops and telling them what to do to please the gods in heaven. Whenever there was trouble at Ife, he would consult the oracle to find out what sacrifices to offer to the gods in heaven so that peace might return to the land.

It happened that at that time at Ife, there was great famine. The rains had failed and the ground had become so dry and hard that it was not possible to plant any food crops. Food and water became

70

scarce and people began to die of starvation and thirst. The elders of Ife became very worried about the situation in the land, and they went to Orunmila to seek his advice.

Orunmila consulted the oracle and told them to offer sacrifices to the gods in heaven because the gods were angry with them. He said to them, "Go quickly and bring me two hundred bush rats, two hundred fishes, two hundred hens, two hundred pigeons, two hundred she-goats, two hundred he-goats and two hundred of everything found at Ife and I will offer them as sacrifices to the gods in heaven so that they may not come down to destroy you." But the elders of Ife felt that Orunmila was asking for the impossible and they got angry with him and called him a liar. Then they left him.

After they had gone, Orunmila offered a sacrifice to the gods in heaven to find out what he himself should do. The chief of the gods in heaven then spoke to him and said, "The people of Ife always forget us when we make life easy for them. It is then that they begin to misbehave and to commit all sorts of crimes against one another. They cheat, they steal and they kill one another. So we have to punish them to make them mend their ways; and we are going to punish them this time because they have not taken your advice. We therefore order you to return to heaven before we destroy Ife." Orunmila thanked the god for his advice and he immediately brought out his magic rope, hooked it to the sky, and climbed back to heaven on it.

As soon as he had gone, black clouds began to gather and the sky grew dark and ominous; the air became still and there was a strange hush everywhere; not even a leaf rustled on the tree and not even a bird chirped. Moments later, the wind rose and began to howl. A storm broke out and the rain, accompanied by the terrific roar of thunder and lightning, began to fall.

At first, the people were glad because they felt that they would soon be able to plant their seeds after the rain and that they would have food to eat and water to drink. But as the wind mounted to the roar of a hurricane, and the rain began to fall in torrents, the people became afraid. Day in, day out, the rain-storm continued wiping out everything in its path. Soon, the rivers became swollen and overflowed their banks. And still, the rain-storm continued. Gradually, the flood waters began to inch their way into the houses until the houses became flooded and people who were caught inside them, could not escape and they all perished there. And still the rain-storm continued unabated. The flood waters rose higher and higher, leaving a wave of destruction behind. Houses shuddered and rocked before they toppled down. Giant trees were up-rooted and fell with a deafening roar. Men, women and children, beasts, trees and all were drowned. Soon, everything at Ife was gone. And the place became a scene of utter devastation and

desolation.

When everything at Ife had perished, the rain stopped and the sky became clear and bright again. But did I say everything perished? No, not everything. There was one single coconut tree left in the whole of Ife. Then the gods in heaven took one look at Ife and saw the utter destruction and desolation there and they felt sorry for destroying it. So they asked Orunmila to go down once again to Ife to re-create new life there.

Orunmila climbed down from heaven on his magic rope. When he got to Ife and saw the flood waters, he began to wonder where he would stay to begin his work of creation afresh. He looked around and saw the top of a coconut tree showing above the flood waters. Then he cried aloud and said to the coconut tree, "So, you are the only tree alive in the whole of Ife? You surely must be gifted with long life!" Orunmila alighted on top of the coconut tree and from there, began to re-create all things anew at Ife. From that time, Orunmila became known as Agbonniregun, meaning it is the coconut tree that Orunmila, the sun god, climbed.

How Ifa Became a Great Teacher

Once upon a time, in the ancient city of Ife, there lived a man whose name was Ifa. He was a poor beggar. He always wore dirty rags and his head was always unshaven. He looked so wretched and so wild that many people thought he was mad. Everyday, in sunshine and in rain, Ifa trudged through the streets of Ife crying, "In the name of Olodumare, the creator of all things, give a poor man something to eat." When people heard his voice, they would say, "Here comes the mad man, let us give him food so that he would go away quickly." Then they would give him corn, fried bean-cakes and other food-stuffs which they could spare. Sometimes, when he was lucky, they gave him cowrie shells to buy whatever he liked.

But as time went on, people got tired of giving him food. Then they began to drive him away whenever he asked them for alms. They were unkind to him and called him the unlucky one. Very often, he would return to his hut in the bush, hungry and tired. He was miserable and often wished he were dead. He often thought about what to do to improve his lot, but he found no answer to his problems.

Ifa used to spend many days and nights in his hut praying to the gods of his fathers to help him out of his misery. One day, whilst he was praying, he fell asleep and had a very strange dream. In his dream, a man who looked like one of the gods in heaven appeared to him and said, "Ifa, get up and listen to me; your prayers are heard, and I am sent from heaven to help you. I will teach you what work to do to make you rich and famous and you will no longer have to trudge through the streets of Ife, begging for food. Instead, people from all over the world will come to seek your help and bring you gifts. You will also become a great teacher and your pupils will come from all over the world. They will include kings, princes, noble-men, priests, traders and men from all walks of life. Your name will become a household word in all the land." Then the strange man brought out what looked like sixteen palm-nuts from his pocket and showed them to Ifa and told him that the sixteen palm-nuts represented the sixteen spirits that controlled men's fortune on earth. He called the palm-nuts *odus* and he taught Ifa the special name by which each one of the odus was known in heaven. He called the first odu *Ejiogbe* and he called the sixteenth and last odu *Ofun*. He told him that these two were the most important odus and that they must be respected at all times. Then he taught Ifa how to use the sixteen odus to find answers to all the problems that beset human beings. It did not matter how difficult the problem was, the odus, because they represented spirits, would solve it. After teaching him all he ought to know about these palm-nuts, the strange man tied a magic string round Ifa's wrist so that Ifa might not forget everything he had learnt in his dream when he woke up. He also gave him the sixteen palm-nuts. Then the strange man disappeared and Ifa woke up.

At first, Ifa was worried and frightened by his dream. He could not understand the strange appearance of the man in his dream although he remembered very clearly everything the man taught him. He also saw the magic string tied round his wrist and the sixteen palm-nuts lying on the floor of his hut. Surely, this cannot be an ordinary dream, said Ifa to himself. See the string round my wrist! And I remember everything so clearly! Yes, I do. Sixteen palm-nuts called odus. Each one has a special name, the names of spirits! . . . Let me see; what are the names? . . . Yes, I remember them; Ejiogbe and Ofun, the first and the last command great respect! Ha, Ha, ha! and these palm-nuts will tell me the answer to any question which anyone may ask me. . . ha, ha, ha!. . . I can see now that I, Ifa, the poor mad man will become rich at last!

When Ifa had finished talking to himself, he took the sixteen palm-nuts and used them exactly in the way in which he had been taught to use them in his dream. He asked questions and he got answers to them by the different patterns which the palm-nuts formed when he cast them on the ground like dice. Ifa knew then that his dream was true. He no longer went into the street to beg for food because the odus told him where to get everything he needed for himself.

Soon, the people in the town began to wonder what had happened to Ifa because they had not seen him in the streets begging for food. Some thought he had died whilst others thought he must have left the town. So they went into his hut to find out what had happened to him. When they got there, they found him looking comfortable and well fed. He was no longer wearing rags or looking dirty and unkempt.

They were very surprised to see him looking so well. Ifa then invited them to come inside his hut. He told them to ask him any question which they liked and that he would answer it. And so they did. To their great surprise, Ifa gave them the correct answers to all their questions. They could not understand what change had come over him. When they left his hut, they all started to talk and to argue about him until they got home. Some said that he was a god who had only been pretending all the time to be a poor beggar. Others said that some great spirit must have taught him all he knew. But whatever it was they thought about him, only one thing was certain, and that was that Ifa had come into possession of some strange powers.

The story of Ifa's strange powers soon spread throughout the land and people flocked to him to seek his advice. Kings, princes, chiefs, noble-men, priests, traders, both young and old, went to see him, begging him to solve their problems for them. When anyone was sick, his relations would go to Ifa to find out how best to cure him. When a king wanted to go to war, he would go to Ifa to find out if he would win the war. When a girl wanted to get married, her mother would go to Ifa to find out whether the marriage would be a happy one. When they came to see him, they brought him presents. And Ifa helped them all. His sixteen odus gave him all the answers to their problems. He then became rich because of the many gifts he received from his clients. Soon, people gave him other names by which they still call him today. Some called him Agbonniregun whilst others called him Orunmila, which means 'Heaven alone knows who will be saved.'

As time went on, people from far and near began to come to him to learn from him. So he became their teacher. He taught them the secrets of how to use the sixteen odus but he warned them not to disclose these secrets to anybody but an initiate. Up till now, the pupils of Ifa who are called Ifa priests, guard the secrets of Ifa jealously.

Ifa lived to a good old age. When he died, his pupils gave him a grand funeral. Later, after some years, he was regarded as the oracle which everyone must consult on important matters. He became the chief oracle of the Yorubas, just as the Greek god Apollo was the chief oracle whom the Greeks of old went to consult at Delphos. His pupils became very many and they began to hold their meetings in secret, in a forest called the forest of Ifa.

The Monkey With Sixteen Tails

Once upon a time, there lived a hunter. He was a very brave hunter who used to go into the forest of ghosts and strange animals to hunt. One day, he went to tell the king of his country that the next time he went into the forest of ghosts and strange animals to hunt, he would bring the king a monkey with sixteen tails. "What! a monkey with sixteen tails?" said the astonished king. "Whoever told you about such a creature?" But the hunter kept on promising that he would bring the king a monkey with sixteen tails. So the king said to him, "Very well then; if you bring me a monkey with sixteen tails, I shall give you half of my kingdom; but if you don't fulfil your promise, I shall behead you, for coming here to tell tales." The hunter agreed and left the king.

When he reached home, he began to prepare for the hunting expedition into the forest of ghosts where monkeys with many tails live. He brought out his hunting kit and put inside it some food, a cake of black soap, some evil smelling ointment and his bow and arrows. Then he wore his hunting dress which consisted of a pair of short trousers and a black tunic into which had been stitched cowrie-shells and charms to protect him against all evil in the forest. He slung his kit across his shoulder and after he had done this, he set out for the forest of ghosts where the strange monkeys lived.

He got into the forest at night when all the monkeys and all the other animals that lived there had
gone to sleep.

Only the ghosts were awake but they did not take
any notice of him because they were having a feast
and were busy dancing and making merry. So the
hunter quietly slipped into a small clearing he found
in the forest and decided to stay there until the next
morning. Here, he thought of a plan to trick the
monkeys when they came out in the morning to
collect nuts. He took off his tunic and rubbed his
body with the evil smelling ointment so that he
smelt like someone who had died a long time ago.
Then he put on his tunic again. Next, he threw his
bow and arrows to a little distance and then lay
down on the ground as though he were dead. The
evil smelling ointment attracted flies and insects
to him but he did nothing to drive them away. He
just lay down there like a corpse.

In the morning, the monkeys came out to collect nuts. The first monkey that saw the hunter lying on the ground was a monkey with one tail. He
moved cautiously towards him and took a good
look at him. He saw that he did not move at all.
He also saw his bow and arrows lying on the
ground a little further away from him. So he called
to his friend, a monkey with two tails, to come and
look at a dead hunter who had thrown away his
bow and arrow.

When the monkey with two tails came, he also

took a good look at the hunter lying still on the ground and said, "You are right; he is dead and he is already beginning to smell. Look at the flies and the insects crawling all over him. He is surely dead." The two monkeys then began to examine the hunter. They walked round him twice, pulled his legs and arms but he did not move. Then they jumped over him and started beating a tatoo on his stomach with their feet. But still the hunter did not move.

When they had satisfied themselves that the hunter was really dead, they decided to go and call other monkeys to come and see him. The monkey with two tails was the first to start calling out and singing to a monkey with three tails to come out and see the dead hunter. The monkey with three tails came and saw the hunter and he too began to call out to other monkeys to come and see the hunter.

To cut a long story short, each monkey, in turn, called to another monkey with one more tail, to come and see the hunter until the monkey with sixteen tails came. When he got there, he took a good look at the hunter and laughed and said, "How awful you smell! See how flies and insects crawl all over you! Why don't you get up now and kill them, you foolish man who always come to trouble us. Now that you are dead and helpless, I am going to jump on you and use your stomach as my drum, ha, ha, ha."

And so he jumped on the hunter But as soon as he began to stamp his feet on the stomach of the hunter, the hunter suddenly opened his eyes and with his hands, he quickly grabbed the legs of the monkey with the sixteen tails. The hunter held on tightly to the monkey so that he could not escape. When the hunter got up, he picked up his hunting bag and opened it and quickly threw the terrified monkey with the sixteen tails inside it and closed the bag tightly again. He slung the bag on his shoulder, picked up his bow and arrows and set out for home, rejoicing that his mission was successful. On the way, he came to a stream and he stopped there to wash with the soap he had brought with him so as to take away the smell from him. After his bath, he continued his journey home. It was already dark before he got home and so he decided to wait until the next morning before he went to see the king.

Very early in the morning of the following day, the hunter rose, had another bath and changed into his beautifully hand-woven embroidered silk *agbada* robe. Then he took the bag containing the monkey with sixteen tails and went to the king's palace to tell the king he had brought the monkey with sixteen tails.

The king could not believe his ears when he heard the news. So he sent for his bell-man whom he commanded to go and ring the royal bell in the town to summon all the people to the king's square in front of the palace. The bell-man went and did as he was told and before long, all the chiefs and elders and people had assembled in the king's square. Then the king came out and took his place among his people. He sat on his throne. When they had all settled down, the king commanded the hunter to present him with the monkey with sixteen tails or forfeit his life.

Quickly the hunter stepped forward, gathered his robe about him and prostrated in an act of salutation before the king. He said to the king, ''O king, may you live for ever; may the crown stay long on your head; may the shoe stay long on your foot; may nothing evil happen to you or your people.'' After this salutation, he got up and went and brought his bag containing the monkey with sixteen tails. Carefully, he opened the bag and holding the monkey tightly by his legs, he brought him out of the bag and presented him to the astonished king.

The monkey was too tired and afraid to fight back. He did not even make any attempt to scratch the king. He just sat quietly on the king's lap whilst the king examined him closely. First, he counted the tails one by one to make sure they were real. When he was satisfied that the monkey had sixteen tails, he picked him up and showed him to all the people assembled in the square. They all went wild with excitement at the sight of this strange creature. They began to hustle and jostle one another in an attempt to get a close look at the monkey with the sixteen tails. They also began to talk in loud voices, and at the same time, about the monkey.

Some said, "Let us keep him with us." Others said, "No, let him go back to where he belongs, he may bring us bad luck." The children said, "Let him play with us and sing and dance for us; let him wag his tails for us."

When all the excitement had died down, the king called the hunter and praised him for his bravery in daring to go into the forest of ghosts to bring the monkey. So he gave him half of his kingdom. "But," he said to the hunter, "we would not know how to look after a monkey with sixteen tails for we have never seen one before; this one may even be a god disguised as a monkey; for these gods sometimes play tricks with us human beings! Now that we have seen him, I command that you take him back to the forest and release him there so that he can go back and join his friends."

The hunter thanked the king for his generous gifts to him and offered to take the monkey back to the forest. On his way back to the forest, a large crowd of children followed him, singing and dancing all the time:

"O monkey with sixteen tails
Come quickly, come quickly
Come quickly and see a dead hunter
Whose bow and arrows are lying on the ground."

The Tortoise and the Dry Bone

Have you met the tortoise of Yoruba folk tales? Let me introduce him to you. He is the greedy man who always carries his house on his back. He is clever, he is cunning, he is crafty. He is a clown and a jester. He is full of boasts and is the greatest tale bearer on earth. He is curious and never minds his own business. He is wise in his own eyes and pretends to know the answers to all problems. He is a rogue and a villain. He is unruly; he is amusing. You can't help hating him but you can't also stop loving him because he makes you laugh at his folly. His curiosity is never satisfied and this has led him into many adventures which have landed him in serious trouble and for which he is always executed. But the tortoise of Yoruba folk tales never dies. Each time he is put to death, he rises again to continue his life of adventure. He is a married man and his ever faithful and loving wife is *Yannibo*. Here is a story about one of his escapades.

One day, the tortoise went for a walk in the forest. When he got to a clearing in the forest, he saw a dry bone on the ground. Instead of going his way, his curiosity prompted him to stop to examine the dry bone. As he was looking at it, he began to talk to it. He said to it, "Dry bone, dry bone, who turned you into a dry bone? Were you a goat or a cow or a bat before you became a dry bone? Perhaps you were a villain that got executed?

But whatever you were before, doesn't really matter for I can help you to become what you were before. I am the master of the impossible.''

But the dry bone did not answer him. So he shrugged his shoulders and said to the dry bone again, ''Well, if you aren't going to cooperate with me, I can't help you. I am going my way. You can lie down there for ever, you stupid ugly good-for-nothing dry bone.''

The tortoise was just about to leave the dry bone when it began to speak. It said, ''Mr. Tortoise, go away and mind your own business and keep away from trouble.'' The tortoise exclaimed, ''So dry bones do speak? I never knew that they do speak; I was only joking when I was asking you those questions. I never expected you to answer them. But, now I know better. Dry bones do speak. Thank you very much for teaching me that. Now I can leave you. I am going my way to tell the whole world that dry bones do speak.'' So laughing and joking, the tortoise left the dry bone and went his way.

As soon as the tortoise got home, he went straight to the king's palace to tell the king that dry bones do speak. When he got there, he met the king and his chiefs holding a meeting. Without waiting to be invited in by the king, he forced his way in and in a loud voice said to the king and the chiefs. ''I have strange news for you all. I have seen what you have never seen before and I have heard what

you have never heard. I have come to tell you that dry bones do speak; and that one has just spoken to me in the forest today.''

The king and the chiefs were very angry with the tortoise for coming in to disturb their meeting, and for coming to tell tales. The king immediately summoned his guards to come and take the tortoise away and put him in prison. But the guards could not overpower him as he kept on struggling and shouting at the top of his voice, "Dry bones do speak; dry bones do speak. Give me a chance to prove to you that dry bones do speak. If I fail to prove it then you can put me to death." "Very well," said the king, ' I will give you the chance to prove it. But if you fail, you will be put to death for being a nuisance and a foolish tale bearer.'' The king then commanded his guards to follow the tortoise to the forest where dry bones speak.

The guards followed the tortoise to where the dry bone that spoke to him in the forest was. When they got there, the tortoise addressed the dry bone. He said, "Dry bone, dry bone, tell my friends, the king's guards, what you told me before.'' But the dry bone did not speak. "Don't be shy," pleaded the tortoise, "they won't hurt you; they only want to help you, they want to hear you speak.'' But still there was no reply from the dry bone. The tortoise then got angry with the dry bone and began to curse it and to call it names, telling it that it was an ungrateful wretch. But still the dry bone kept mute.

Then the guards got angry with the tortoise for daring to take them on a fool's errand. They were going to bind him hand and foot and take him back to the palace to be executed when he pleaded with them to give him one more chance to speak to the dry bone. He begged them to move away from where the dry bone was because, according to him, the dry bone had refused to speak because it was shy. So the guards gave the tortoise this last chance to prove that the dry bone could speak. They walked a little away from the tortoise and the dry bone.

As soon as they had gone, the dry bone began to speak to the tortoise, saying "I see that you have not heeded my advice; you have not been minding your own business; you have been telling tales. Now you have to suffer for being a tale bearer." When the dry bone was speaking, the tortoise quickly called the guards back to come and listen to the dry bone. But as soon as they came, the dry bone stopped talking and kept mute again. The guards then arrested the tortoise, bound him hand and foot and took him to the king. The king was so angry with him for telling lies that he ordered his immediate execution.

The tortoise now learnt the bitter lesson that one should always mind one's business and go one's way, but it was too late to save him.

The Singing Mushroom

Long, long ago, there lived two brothers who were professional dancers. One day, they went to the next village to dance at the festival of the gods taking place there. On arrival, they found that all the villagers had assembled in an open space in front of the chief's house, waiting for them. So, without wasting time, the elder brother went straight into the centre of the open space and began to dance to entertain the villagers. He danced so well that at the end of the dance, the chief of the village gave him one thousand cowries. He was very pleased with it and thanked the chief for the gift.

Then the younger brother came out to dance. As he was walking towards the centre of the open space, he passed by his elder brother who quietly said to him, "I doubt whether you will get anything today; you are not as good a dancer as I am." But his brother took no notice of him. He just went into the centre of the open space and began to dance. At first, he danced a slow, gentle measure. Then all of a sudden, the rhythm of the drumming changed. The drums began to beat faster and faster and the boy changed his steps to suit the faster rhythm of the drums. As he danced on, the boy became animated by the sound of the drums and he danced with all his heart and soul. Legs, arms and muscles moved rhythmically with the fast booming of the drums and his body glistened with perspiration. He danced all the time, like one in a trance.

Soon, the villagers too became excited with the dancing and the drumming and they began to tap their feet and to sway in rhythmic motion to the beating of the drums. They began to clap their hands and to shower praises on the dancer until the drumming suddenly stopped and the dancer stopped dancing. When the excitement had died down among the villagers, the dancer moved to the place where the chief sat and gathering up his *agbada* robe, prostrated before the chief to salute him. The chief was so impressed by the dancing that he said to him, ''Surely the gods have done us a great honour, in sending you here to dance for us at their festival. They have certainly danced for us through you.'' The chief thanked the dancer and gave him a present of two thousand cowries.

But the elder brother became very jealous of his brother, and in anger, got up and shouted, ''What has my brother done to deserve two thousand cowries? I can dance a thousand times better than that!'' And he got up again and began to dance to show that he was a better dancer than his brother. When he had finished, the villagers still said that his brother was a better dancer. But in order to pacify him, they gave him one sheep.

No sooner had he sat down, than the villagers went to the younger brother to ask him to dance for them again. This time, the boy danced so well

94

that the villagers shouted in excitement. "Either you are one of the gods we are honouring today or you have been possessed by one of them! For who else can make you dance like this?" When he had finished dancing, the chief gave him a present of two sheep.

The praises showered on the boy as well as the money and the sheep given to him made his elder brother very angry indeed. But he could not challenge his brother to another dance because it was already getting late and they had to return to their own village before dark. Already, evening was creeping in. Soon, the sun would become a great ball of red in the tropical sky of the village. Soon, the villagers would return to their huts to sleep and darkness would descend suddenly to envelope the village as there is no twilight in the tropics. The eerie birds of the night, as well as the grasshoppers and the crickets and a few stray sheep and goats would take over the place from the dancers and drummers and villagers and gods.

As soon as the two dancing brothers left the village to return home, the elder brother began to plot to kill his brother. When they reached a lonely spot in the bush which separated their own village from the village where they had gone to dance, the elder brother suddenly brought out his club and clubbed his brother to death. Quickly he made a shallow grave and buried his brother there. Then he took his money and sheep and made his way home.

When he reached home, his parents asked him where his brother was. He told them that his brother had decided to spend the night in the village where they had gone to dance and that he would return home the next day. This explanation satisfied his parents. He showed them the presents they gave him in the village where they had gone to dance and they were pleased and congratulated him for having done so well. His parents happily retired to bed to sleep that night, hoping that the next day their younger son would arrive home to show them his own presents.

Early the next day, at cock-crow, their mother set out for their farm to gather vegetables to bring home to cook before her younger son arrived. When she got there, she bent down and began to pick some spinach. As she did so, she suddenly came to a spot where a very big mushroom had sprung up and she decided to pick it too. But as soon as her hands touched the mushroom, the mushroom began to sing this plaintive song:

> "Mother, don't pick it,
> Please don't pick it.
> We danced, danced, danced,
> They gave the elder
> a thousand cowries.
> They gave the younger
> two thousand cowries.

had become a mushroom, they thought.

When they reached home, they decided to question their elder son about the whereabouts of his brother, especially when he still had not returned home. They called him and asked again where his younger brother was. He said he did not know. They asked him why he had not gone back to the village to look for him. He said he was not his brother's keeper. When they saw that he was not being helpful or sympathetic, they asked him to follow them to the farm. So the three of them left for the farm. When they got there, his parents took him to the place where the mushroom grew. He was very surprised to see it and he exclaimed, "Oh, what a big beautiful mushroom this is!" Then his father told him to bend down, and pick it for his mother. As soon as he bent down and touched the mushroom, the mushroom began to sing.

> "Brother don't pick it,
> Please don't pick it.
> We danced, danced, danced.
> They gave the elder a thousand cowries.
> They gave the younger two thousand cowries.
> They gave the elder, one sheep.
> They gave the younger, two sheep.
> The elder grew jealous and killed the younger with his club.
> And made away with his things.
> Oh cruel, cruel brother."

As soon as the mushroom stopped singing, it jumped up from the ground and caught hold of the nose of the elder brother and began to pull it. He pulled it long and hard. And as it did so, it said, "You wicked, wicked brother." Then the mushroom let go the elder brother's nose and suddenly disappeared into the ground and was seen no more.

The elder brother knew that the secret was out, and weeping very loudly, he confessed his guilt to his sorrowful parents. Then they returned home.

When they got home, his father went and told the chief and the elders in their village what his elder son had done to his brother. The chief and the elders were very angry when they heard the report and they immediately sent for the elder brother and told him that a wicked and cruel man like him was not fit to live among human beings, and that he must leave the village at once and never return there again. So they called the villagers together and asked them to chase him out of their village into the forest where he must remain alone until he died. Then the chief and the elders met again and took a vow that nobody must ever use a club to kill his fellow brother again.

CPSIA information can be obtained at www.ICGtesting.com
Printed in the USA
LVOW010333281211

261334LV00005B/9/A